BOUSHRA'S DAY

To all the children of the world, and to Islam,
the religion that taught me how to love and respect others.

Boushra's Day copyright © Frances Lincoln Limited 2002
Text copyright © Dalia Khattab 2002
Photographs copyright © Khaled Eldash 2002
The Publishers would like to acknowledge Prodeepta Das as the originator of the series of which this book forms a part.
Prodeepta Das is the author and photographer of *Geeta's Day*.

First published in Great Britain in 2002 by Frances Lincoln Limited,
4 Torriano Mews, Torriano Avenue, London NW5 2RZ

British Cataloguing in Publication Data available on request

ISBN 0-7112-1931-1

Designed by Sophie Pelham

Printed in Singapore

1 3 5 7 9 8 6 4 2

AUTHOR ACKNOWLEDGEMENTS
With grateful thanks to Boushra and her family.
Thanks also to Okasha El Daly at London University for checking the text.

BOUSHRA'S DAY

From Dawn to Dusk in an Egyptian City

Khaled Eldash and Dalia Khattab

FRANCES LINCOLN

AUTHOR'S NOTE

Boushra Bobbos and her family live in Cairo. Their apartment is only a short walk away from Pyramids Road, which leads out into the desert to the famous Giza Pyramids. Boushra sees the Pyramids every day on her walk to school, so to her they seem almost ordinary. Her father likes to remind her how difficult it must have been for the ancient Egyptians to build them.

AFRICA

Cairo

EGYPT

The Bobbos' apartment is in Faisal Street in an area of Cairo called Giza, which is about half an hour by car from central Cairo. There are lots of shops, restaurants and cafés in Giza, so Boushra only goes into central Cairo for special occasions, like to buy new clothes for Eid al-Fitr, the three-day feast that comes at the end of Ramadan (the Muslim holy month).

About once a week, Boushra and her two little brothers go to one of the cafés in Faisal Street with their mother. Boushra pretends to study the menu but she always has the same thing in the end: a cup of tea and a large slice of creamy chocolate cake.

Boushra is seven years old.

She lives on the third floor of an apartment block in Cairo with her parents and her brothers Ismail and Ihab. Boushra's father works in a local tourist shop, which specialises in souvenirs of ancient Egypt.

On schooldays Boushra sets her alarm for seven o'clock. As soon as she's out of bed, she goes to the bathroom and performs her *wudu*.

WUDU is a special wash that Muslims carry out before praying. First Boushra washes her hands, then her mouth, next her nose (by rinsing water around her nostrils), then her face, arms, head, ears, neck, and finally her feet. She repeats each stage of her wudu three times.

When she has finished, Boushra puts on her veil and says her first prayers of the day. She prays to Allah, the Muslim name for God. Salah (prayer) is the 'second pillar' of Islam. These pillars are like laws, and there are five in all.

Like most people in Egypt, Boushra and her family are Muslim. Muslim people are followers of Islam, one of the world's oldest religions.

When Boushra has changed into her school uniform, her mother calls her into the dining room for breakfast. Today there are all the usual things – bread and cheese, honey, milk and yoghurt. Boushra starts off with a cheese sandwich. Her little brother Ismail has already had his breakfast, and is hiding under the table!

4

Before they leave for school, Boushra's mother brushes Boushra's hair and puts in some colourful ribbons.

5

Boushra says goodbye to her mum and brothers and sets off to school with her father. As they make their way along the busy streets, Boushra points out a large group of tourists. Her father says that they will be good for business because they will all want souvenirs of their trip to the Pyramids.

THE PYRAMIDS of Ancient Egypt were probably built as tombs for the Pharaohs (the kings), to protect them in the life they would have after they died. The three pyramids at Giza are named after the three Pharaohs who were buried inside them: Cheops, Chephren (the one you can see here) and Mycerinus. There is also a large statue at Giza called the Sphinx (which you can see here). The Sphinx has the head of a pharaoh and the body of a lion.

Boushra and her classmates start the day by reciting some verses from the Quran (sometimes it is spelt Koran). The teacher reads out a few lines at a time and then everyone repeats what she has said.

THE QURAN is the sacred book of Islam. Muslim people believe it is the word of Allah, and it gives them guidance throughout their lives.

The next lesson is maths. The teacher begins by asking some simple questions. It's a race to see who can answer first.

Then there are some harder problems to solve. The teacher asks Boushra to come to the board so that the class can see how she works out the answers. Boushra doesn't make any mistakes. She likes numbers and wants to be an accountant when she grows up.

After break, Boushra and her classmates have a music lesson. Boushra's best-friend Hannan is chosen to play the class lute (a wooden stringed instrument, similar to a guitar).

At the end of the lesson, they all sing 'Belady Belady' ('Oh My Country, I Love You'), which is Egypt's national anthem.

Afterwards they go to the library. First they look at picture books and then the teacher reads them the story of Aladdin, who travelled all over the world on his flying carpet.

ALADDIN is the adventurous hero in one of the tales of the Arabian Nights, *a famous collection of 1001 stories written in Arabic.*

11

By half-past twelve, school has already finished for the day, and
Boushra and her mother go to the market to get some vegetables
for lunch. Boushra asks the stallholder for some molokhia (a type
of green leafy vegetable).

Then they go to see Boushra's father at his shop. He is showing a tourist how to make *papyrus* just like they used to in ancient Egypt.

PAPYRUS is made from a reed with a long green stem (also called papyrus). To make the papyrus, Boushra's father cuts the stem into strips, soaks these in water, and then lays the strips on top of each other in a crisscross pattern. He then puts the papyrus under a heavy weight until it is dry and ready to be decorated.

The shop also sells ornamental scarab beetles. In ancient Egypt, scarabs were a symbol of the sun god, and were thought to bring good luck.

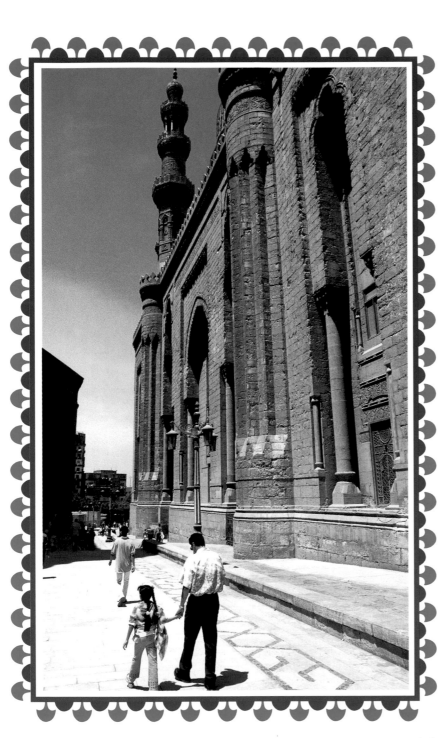

Now it is time for the second prayer of the day, *salat al-zuhr.*

Boushra and her father walk to the mosque. All over Cairo, the streets echo with the sound of the *azzan.*

AZZAN This is the Muslim 'call to prayer'. Each mosque has a muezzin (caller) who goes to the tower of the mosque when it is prayer time and calls the azzan through a loud speaker.

14

Once they are inside, Boushra and her father take off their shoes and begin their prayers. Everyone in the congregation faces in the direction of Mecca, the holy city in Saudi Arabia which is where you can find the *Ka'bah*.

KA'BAH This is the most sacred site for a Muslim. It is believed by Muslims to be the first site of worship. Every Muslim is required to make a journey to Mecca to visit the Ka'bah at least once in their lifetime, if they are able.

15

Afterwards, Boushra's father takes her back to the apartment, where her mother is getting lunch ready. Boushra helps prepare the molokhia they bought earlier at the market.

As well as molokhia soup, they eat fried chicken, rice, bread and mekhalil (green peppers and olives in a vinegar, garlic and salt dressing).

After lunch, Boushra settles down to her Arabic homework. She has to complete two pages of grammar exercises by the start of school on Saturday. Although it is only Thursday, Boushra wants to do it all today so that she can have a free weekend.

In Egypt, the working week begins on Saturday and ends on Thursday. Most people, including Boushra, only have one day (Friday) for their weekend.

17

Boushra knows the weekend has really begun when she gets to her grandmother's house in the evening. Her grandmother has a sugarcane farm by the River Nile, not far from Giza. Boushra and her brother Ihab love sitting by the water and sucking on the sweet sugarcane juice.

Some of the farmers are on their break, and they invite Boushra and Ihab to join them for a glass of tea. The tea is flavoured with mint leaves and they add lots of sugar to it to make it sweet.

Tomorrow is the beginning of Ramadan so in the evening Boushra and her cousins sing 'Ramadan Gana', which means 'Welcome Ramadan'.

RAMADAN is the ninth month of the Muslim calendar. During Ramadan Muslim people obey the fourth pillar of Islam, which is to fast during the hours of daylight.

Boushra misses her grandmother during the week and they always have a lot to catch up on at the weekend. While her grandmother knits, Boushra chats to her about the latest adventures of Bakar, the popular Egyptian cartoon character.

By the time they have reached the end of their ball of wool, Boushra can't stop yawning. She makes her grandmother promise that they will watch an episode of Bakar on television in the morning, and then kisses her good night. *Tisbahi ala kher, Boushra.* (Good night, Boushra.)

23

MORE ABOUT EGYPT

EGYPT, THE PAST

The great civilization that people call 'ancient Egypt' lasted for over four thousand years. Most ordinary Egyptians during this time lived in houses made out of mud and brick, and worked as farmers or craftsmen. The most powerful person in ancient Egypt was the pharaoh (the king), who had immense wealth. The ancient Egyptians worshipped many gods, and they believed that the pharaoh was the representative of all these gods on earth.

The buildings in Egypt tell the story of its history. The pyramids were built by the ancient Egyptians, but later on many beautiful mosques and churches were built by the Islamic and Christian Egyptians.

In 1798, Napoleon and his French army stormed Cairo and fought a bloody battle with the Turkish army who were in charge. The French (like all the countries of Europe) wanted to take control of Egypt so that they could add it to the list of countries they had in their empire.

After the French, the British ruled Egypt for about eighty years. But the Egyptians wanted independence. In 1952 there was a great revolt. The British were forced to withdraw and Egypt at last became an independent country.

EGYPT, THE LAND

An ancient historian once said that 'Egypt is the gift of the Nile'. He said this because Egypt is nearly all desert, and it would be impossible for the country to exist without the water of the River Nile. The Nile flows all the way through the middle of the country. The weather in Egypt is usually hot and dry. Egyptians don't have central heating in their homes because there is no need for it, even in the winter months.

PEOPLE IN EGYPT

Egyptians are very cheerful people. One of the things they like to do most is listen to music. If you came to visit Boushra in Cairo, you would hear music everywhere – in the shops, on the streets and in the taxis. People are always humming along to a tune. One of Egypt's most popular singers was a woman called Umm Kolthum.

Drinking tea and coffee is another favourite Egyptian pastime. Egyptian men in particular like nothing better than an afternoon at their local *ahwa* (coffeehouse), reading the paper and playing dominoes with their friends.

RELIGION IN EGYPT

Most Egyptian people are Muslim (which means they follow Islam) but there are also many Christians who live in Egypt.

The religion of Islam was revealed over a thousand years ago to a man called Mohammed. When Mohammed was about forty years old, Allah (God) began talking to him. Mohammed is called a 'Prophet' because he was Allah's messenger on earth. All Allah's teachings are written down in the Quran, which is the holy book of Islam.

THE FIVE PILLARS OF ISLAM
Muslims have to:

1. Declare that there is no God but Allah and that Mohammed is his Prophet
2. Pray five times a day
3. Give money to the needy
4. Fast during Ramadan
5. Make a pilgrimage (a religious journey) to Mecca – as long as they can afford it and are in good health

LANGUAGE IN EGYPT

The official language of Egypt is Arabic. There are 28 letters in the Arabic alphabet and they look very different from English letters – the letter 'b', for example, is written as B, and the letter 'g' is written as J. (The Arabic words in this book have been specially written using the English alphabet so that you can read them.) Arabic also sounds different from English, and can be difficult for English speakers to pronounce.

The Arabic of the Quran, and the Arabic that is written in the Egyptian newspapers and spoken on the radio is called 'classical' Arabic. The Egyptian Arabic that people use to talk to their friends and family is less formal. Sometimes it's hard to believe it's the same language!

Most people in ancient Egypt could not read or write. They relied on a small group of men called 'scribes' to do it for them. The scribes wrote in pictures, called hieroglyphs. For a long time, modern language experts couldn't work out what the hieroglyphs meant. They had to wait until the Rosetta Stone was discovered in 1799 to unlock the key to this ancient language. The Rosetta Stone is engraved with three passages of writing, including one passage in hieroglyphs. The French scholar Jean-Francois Champollion realised that each passage of writing had the same meaning – so by comparing all three, he was able to work out what each hieroglyph meant. It was a very exciting discovery.

SOME EGYPTIAN ARABIC WORDS AND PHRASES

salam alekum – hello

maas salama – goodbye

shukran – thank you

aywa – yes

Izzayyak? – How are you? (when asking a girl)

Izzayyik? – How are you? (when asking a boy)

GLOSSARY

ahwa – a traditional Egyptian coffeehouse. Ahwa is also the word for 'coffee'

Aladdin – a character from the Arabian Nights

Allah – God

Arabian Nights – a collection of folk tales, written in Arabic. It is also known as the *Thousand and One Nights*

azzan – the Muslim call to prayer

Bakar – a popular Egyptian cartoon character who has many adventures around the tombs of Upper Egypt (southern Egypt)

'Belady Belady' – the Egyptian national anthem

Cheops – an ancient Egyptian king. The Pyramid of Cheops at Giza is the largest pyramid in Egypt. It took about thirty years to build and was completed around 2600 BC

Chephren – the son of King Cheops. The Pyramid of Chephren is one of the three Giza Pyramids

Eid al-Fitr – the three-day feast that comes at the end of the Ramadan fast

Ka'bah – a Muslim holy site in Mecca

mekhalil – a dish of green peppers and olives in a garlicky dressing

Mohammed – the Prophet to whom the religion of Islam was revealed

molokhia – a green leafy vegetable

muezzin – the official of the mosque who calls people to prayer from the minaret (the tower of the mosque)

Mycerinus – King Mycerinus was the son of King Chephren and the grandson of King Cheops. The Pyramid of Mycerinus is the smallest of the three Giza Pyramids

papyrus – the paper they used to make from papyrus reed in ancient Egypt

Quran – the holy book of Islam

Ramadan – the ninth month of the Muslim calendar, when Muslim people fast during the day. At this time of year, all the children sing 'Ramadan Gana', which means 'Welcome Ramadan'

salah – prayer. Muslims are expected to pray five times every day

salat al-zuhr – the second prayer of the Muslim day

scarab – a sacred symbol in ancient Egypt

Tisbahi ala kher, Boushra – Good night, Boushra

wudu – the ritual cleansing that Muslims have to carry out before prayer

INDEX